ROWvotions
Volume II

ROWvotions
Volume II

✦

The devotional book of
Rivers of the World

Ben Mathes with Karin M. Clack

iUniverse, Inc.

New York Lincoln Shanghai

ROWvotions Volume II
The devotional book of Rivers of the World

iUniverse books may be ordered through booksellers or by contacting:

iUniverse
2021 Pine Lake Road, Suite 100
Lincoln, NE 68512
www.iuniverse.com
1-800-Authors (1-800-288-4677)

ISBN-13: 978-0-595-43261-5 (pbk)
ISBN-13: 978-0-595-87602-0 (ebk)
ISBN-10: 0-595-43261-1 (pbk)
ISBN-10: 0-595-87602-1 (ebk)

Printed in the United States of America

Cover design by Liz Alderman, www.lizaldermandesign.com

Contents

Foreword

Since 1978, Dr. Ben Mathes has been traveling the world on behalf of our Lord. His ministry has taken him to over 50 countries. Currently the president of Rivers of the World (ROW), Dr. Mathes helps to provide people, money, and other items to reach the world's poorest with a ministry of compassion and hope.

When in the States, Dr. Mathes speaks in almost 200 cities a year. His radio ministry reaches over 3 million listeners in 48 states.

These devotions are based on his radio ministry.

To contact ROW and Dr. Mathes:

www.row.org

Dr. Ben C. Mathes
PMB 64
6625 Hwy. 53 East, Suite 410
Dawsonville, Ga. 30534

706-344-1283

Ben@row.org

Preface

The very hand of God orchestrated this book of devotions. It is an answer to several years of prayer in which I asked the Lord to give me an opportunity to write solely for Him. As a newspaper reporter, I am often restricted with limitations on voicing my Christian views. I have desired for some time to use the gift of writing He has blessed me with so that I may bless others in the furtherance of His kingdom.

Earlier this year, I had heard several radio spots featuring Rivers of the World on a contemporary Christian radio station. One evening after I browsed the ROW web site I decided to send an e-mail volunteering my services to the organization for proofreading or editing materials.

Within a few days, ROW President Ben Mathes replied to my e-mail noting it was an answer to their prayers as they were looking for someone to take their radio spots and create articles for future publications. I immediately saw God's hand in the midst of this awesome opportunity.

I gathered some of my previous newspaper articles, e-mailed them as samples of my work and within a day my journey as a freelance "ghost" writer had begun.

These devotions have given me a chance to allow the Holy Spirit to inspire me and to let His words flow through me. I hope the devotions will touch the hearts and lives of people in need of the Savior or those who simply desire a closer walk with Jesus.

Much prayer takes place before words are placed on a page. These prayers include asking Him to give to me the right words to make an impact upon others and for Him to guide me to the specific Scripture He would have me to incorporate in each devotion.

I humbly thank my Lord for His daily presence in my life and for allowing me to be His instrument to reach a lost and dying world for Him. If but one soul accepts salvation because of these devotions, then I have fulfilled my mission.

There is another spirit that nudges me to take my thoughts and carefully and creatively arrange them on paper so that others may be inspired and blessed. Her name is Anna W. King, my dear grandmother whose written words were silenced in the fall of 1997 as her Lord called her home. She still gives me inspiration and I hope I can continue to "speak" for her until my Lord calls me home.

To God be the glory.

Karin M. Clack
Wilkesboro, NC

Acknowledgements

I am so grateful that the Lord has enabled me to experience so many things in so many places! Christian missions are exciting to say the least! My heartfelt thanks and prayers go to my wife, Dr. Mickie Mathes, for her courage; to "3," for running ROW with a gentle spirit; to Liz Alderman, our graphic designer, for capturing the essence of ROW in her work; to Karin Clack, whose writing skills shine in each devotion; to Winston, my dog; and to all who make ROW possible. God bless you!

Ben C. Mathes
Dawsonville, Ga.

Always in Season

The most eloquently wrapped presents and the most expensive gifts are not the ones that leave a lasting impression upon us at Christmastime. Often, the very small "gifts" have the most meaning.

I was speaking to an elementary school in southern Atlanta and I mentioned to the class that one of my friends is a general who is a rebel leader in the civil war in the Congo. The children and teachers were amazed so I pulled out my cell phone and called the general.

At first, the teachers really didn't believe me until I handed the phone to one of the teachers. She was able to speak to the general, who reminded the children to stay in school. As he was speaking to the teacher, I got the children ready to present the general with Christmas wishes. As I handed the phone to the children, they sang, "We wish you a Merry Christmas and a Happy New Year."

As I got back on the phone, all I could hear was silence. The next thing I heard was the general weeping over the joy and love of these precious children for the small, but wonderful "gift" they gave to him that Christmas season.

We are reminded in Galatians 5:22-23, "But the fruit of the Spirit is love, joy, peace, patience, kindness, goodness, faithfulness, gentleness and self-control …"

As a Christian, these virtues should not be individual traits that we possess from time to time. Instead, these Christ-like qualities must be woven together, with love being at the root of them all.

Sharing our joy with others, showering someone with kindness and possessing a gentle spirit are gifts we can exchange with others year-round.

Be Clothed in Kindness

Many of us have seen the nightly news recently, or read the headlines in the newspapers about the marches taking place nationwide protesting against proposed changes in immigration. Tensions have flared as some folks have loudly stated their opinions about people who have come to the United States from other countries, either legally or illegally.

Through my travels with Rivers of the World (ROW), I have been exposed to many cultures in numerous foreign countries. On a recent trip traveling across Central America, I arrived in the country late and spent the night in a hotel. I awoke the next morning and boarded a bus across the country, which I had never done before.

I stopped in a hotel, got a room and got something to eat. All along the way, these simple tasks were complicated by the fact that I don't speak the native language very well. However, at every turn I met a stranger who offered assistance with getting on the bus, finding a hotel room and pointing me in the right direction for a place to eat. I was a foreigner, yet I was greeted with much kindness.

Let us follow the instructions in Colossians 3:12, which says, "Therefore, as God's chosen people, holy and dearly loved, clothe yourselves with compassion, kindness, humility, gentleness and patience."

We are very diligent in selecting the clothes we will wear each day to work, school or elsewhere. Are we equally as diligent in clothing ourselves each day in the likeness of Christ, with love, compassion and kindness? Regardless of your circumstances today and in spite of the people who may cross your path today, greet everyone this day in kindness.

Be On Guard

I admit it ... three of my least favorite words are, "Hey, wake up!" We all experience periods in our lives where we receive a "wake up call."

My young friend, Robert, is a Marine serving in Iraq. He described to me the day that three mortar rounds were fired by the enemy, landing right beside him. Two of the mortar rounds were duds, thank God. The third mortar round exploded. Robert escaped injury from all the shrapnel but two of his friends were wounded.

Robert said that was a wake up call for him. He decided he needed to sit down with Dr. Chris Price, my dear friend, and share his life and realign himself with the love and grace of God.

As you wake up today, sip your coffee and watch the beauty of the sun rising, I encourage you to see, hear, feel, smell and touch the very blessings of God. Thank Him that His mercies are indeed new every morning. Thank Him too for living in America where we are still free to worship and praise Him.

As Christians, we must never lay our guard down or get too comfortable in our walk with the Lord. Christ instructs us in 1 Peter 5:8-9, "Be self-controlled and alert. Your enemy the devil prowls around like a roaring lion looking for someone to devour. Resist him, standing firm in the faith, because you know that your brothers throughout the world are undergoing the same kind of sufferings."

We may not want to admit it, but it is true, the devil is always on the prowl looking for ways to infiltrate into the lives of Christians—all he needs is a weak area. We take time each day to dress a certain way for whatever activity we have planned. We must also take time each day to put on the full armor of God so we can resist the temptations of the devil. Be vigilant, alert today, and pray for fellow Christians so they also may remain strong in the Lord.

Blessed Beyond Measure

In today's busy society where many businesses are now open 24 hours a day, I can imagine some of you are either getting ready to go to the grocery store or have just arrived home from buying groceries. We don't think much about this convenience. Yet, grocery stores are scarce in many countries where most people swap and sell produce and other items at open-air markets.

While in Bangladesh, I met a man who had 21 people in his family and who only had three acres of land to farm. It doesn't take much thought, time or resources to give a person food to feed their family. However, this is only a temporary fix to a more serious problem. It requires far more time, effort and resources to teach a man to provide for his family for years to come.

ROW staff and volunteers were able to teach this man how to grow a balanced diet on his land. With this new skill, he was able to feed his family 11 months out of the year without needing a second job. He was so appreciative that he wanted to demonstrate his gratitude by giving me a huge coconut to drink. I accepted his generosity and drank the coconut.

The man then gave me a second coconut, which I managed to spill down the front of my shirt. He tried to give me yet another coconut and I had to finally say, "That is it! I can't take anymore!"

Sometimes in our walk with the Lord, Christ blesses us in the same manner—to overflowing and we are so overwhelmed by His blessings to the point where we too feel like saying, "Enough! I can't take anymore!"

God is faithful to His word when He says in Psalm 107:9, "He satisfies the thirsty and fills the hungry with good things."

God not only satisfies us with material blessings and by meeting our daily needs, He also fills us to overflowing with His wonderful Holy Spirit who satisfies the very longings of our hearts.

Calm in the Storm

It is a pretty summer day as you are taking a drive, listening to some uplifting music and all of a sudden you see them ... flashing blue lights in your rear view mirror. You pull over, come to a complete stop and your heart is racing. There just isn't anything more frightening than that, is there?

While traveling the Sankuru River in the Congo we experienced a far more frightening situation than being pulled over by a police officer. We were traveling in a loaded dug out canoe with a small outboard motor when soldiers suddenly poured out of the forest. The soldiers had abandoned their uniforms, but not their weapons.

With guns raised, the soldiers screamed for us to come back. Very carefully, we turned our canoe around as fear gripped us. Thankfully, Umba, with his gentle and kind spirit, was able to smooth out this dangerous situation.

The Lord is also gentle and kind and always with us. No matter our troubles and no matter our challenges, the Lord will stay with us and be with us through the most difficult times of our lives.

He gives us this promise in Psalm 116:5-6, "The LORD is gracious and righteous; our God is full of compassion. The Lord protects the simplehearted; when I was in great need, he saved me."

Computers—An Effective Tool in Evangelism

Used correctly, computers and Christianity can be completely compatible. Over the years, we have discovered that young people all over the world want to learn computer skills, they want to learn English and they want to study Scripture.

To combine all three areas, we have created computer schools in areas such as Kenya, the Dominican Republic, Peru and in Belize at the New Life School, located in Orange Walk. To date, we've created around eight computer schools, which allow the children to develop computer skills, learn English and study Scripture.

There are certainly many sinful and evil aspects associated with computers, especially the Internet. However, when Christians who have a heart for God are able to combine the technology of computers with evangelism, it can be a very effective tool in reaching the lost for Christ.

Think about it … how does using your computer daily affect your faith? Do you lift up fellow Christians by sending e-mails letting them know you are praying for them? As you are surfing the Internet, do you visit Christian ministry web sites? Teaching a child how to use a computer properly, teaching them how to communicate effectively in English and their native language, then incorporating Christianity, can be a powerful tool for witnessing.

Christ tells us in Mark 16:15 to, "Go into all the world and preach the good news to all creation."

What better way to reach the entire world with the good news of Christ than through computers? There are those whose ministry is to be a missionary to areas around the world. We are not all called to be missionaries, but we are all called to share the good news of salvation to all creation. Let us use this tool of technology to make a difference for Christ.

Dedicating Our All to Him

Have you ever seen a ship christened? This is when a ceremony is held complete with a bottle of champagne that is whacked across the side of a ship. Earlier this year, my wife, Mickie, christened our newest ship based in the Congo.

In her best French, Mickie said, "I dedicate this ship to Jesus Christ and I name her *Mama Mickie.*"

I can't imagine all the lives that will be touched by the ministry of that new ship as it cruises down the Sankuru River delivering medical supplies and much needed hope. Here, in America, many of us own our own homes, virtually all of us have vehicles and some folks have numerous material possessions.

I wonder how many of us have taken the time, not to christen necessarily, but to dedicate our homes, our cars and our possessions to the ministry of Jesus Christ. Many Christians may falsely believe that only missionaries who dedicate their lives to the ministry of Christ are called to make many sacrifices, including leaving behind homes, families and the comforts of living in America. Christ has commissioned all Christians to go out into "the highways and hedges and compel them to come in." (Luke 14:23)

I ask you today, have you dedicated your car, your home, your family and yourself to the service of the Lord? We must reach a place in our lives where we realize all that we possess and all of who we are belongs to Jesus.

Every Second Counts

Have you ever stopped to think about the suffering that occurs in just a minute of time? A minute is not long. It is merely 60 seconds. However, did you realize that every minute two children die of Malaria in Africa? Every 60 seconds 10 people are infected with HIV. Three people die every minute of tuberculosis. One pregnant woman dies every 60 seconds from complications.

These are examples of needless and unnecessary suffering that occurs in our world, in a span of just 60 seconds.

I challenge you today to examine how you use every minute of each day the Lord provides for you. Go a step further and think about the decisions you make each day and how those decisions could be aligned with the will of God to help change the world for Jesus Christ.

These are not difficult things for us to do if we would first come before the throne of God in heartfelt prayer seeking to know more of Him and desiring to be led by the Holy Spirit.

Too often, we fail to realize the genuine gift each day is and we carelessly go through life as if we have all the time in the world.

We are warned in James 4:13-15, "Now listen, you who say, 'Today or tomorrow we will go to this or that city, spend a year there, carry on business and make money.' Why, you do not even know what will happen tomorrow. What is your life? You are a mist that appears for a little while and then vanishes. Instead, you ought to say, 'If it is the Lord's will, we will live and do this or that.'"

As we arise to greet this day, let us remember that this may be our last chance to make a difference in someone's life for Christ's sake.

Feasting at His Table

I just love to eat! I especially enjoy going to the grocery store, buying some food, coming home and rustling up a bunch of grub!

We recently took my wife, Mickie, shopping in the Congo. In some of the open markets there you can buy everything imaginable to eat. There are live termites, caterpillars, big maggots, smoked monkeys and some animal that the locals call a ground hog. If you buy meat in one of these markets make sure it is fresh because it is usually slaughtered right there on the spot.

We bought pots and pans, utensils, spices and oils then we spent all day cooking up a feast. All of our staff gathered around the table as we gave thanks for the food before us. It was quite a celebration!

The next time you approach the Lord's table, think about what it took to prepare that meal. Regardless if you have steak to eat tonight or simply milk and bread, focus upon the One who provided not only the food that you have to eat, but also gave His body and poured out His blood for the sins of all mankind.

In Luke 22:19-20 (KJV), Jesus is sharing in His last meal with His disciples as He took the bread, gave thanks to His Father and broke it. When Jesus gave the bread to the disciples He said, "This is my body which is given for you: this do in remembrance of me." Jesus then took the cup after supper and said, "This cup is the new testament in my blood, which is shed for you."

Whether we are eating a meal, serving a meal to others or doing some other ministry for the Lord, let us sacrifice our all for Him who gave His all for us. Feast at His table today and consume all the blessings He has for you—peace, joy, a passion for the lost, grace, a clean heart and an insatiable appetite for more of Him.

Get Off the Sidelines

Everything we do has occupational hazards associated with it. One of the hazards I face in my travels around the world are diseases and parasites.

Shortly after I arrived home from a trip to Africa, I noticed some worms were growing in my arm. Carefully and diligently, I was able to remove four of the five worms from my arm. The fifth worm made his appearance when I was speaking to a high school in Augusta, Ga. He was removed from my arm and if you stop by the biology lab, you will find a jar labeled "Ben" that has my worm.

About now you are probably thinking, "Oh, my gosh, he had worms coming out of his arm! How disgusting!"

Having parasites in your body or being infected by a disease while serving God in remote corners of the world might not be your definition of following after Christ. However, we are not going to solve problems in this world unless we are willing to get in the midst of the problems and "get dirty." This includes worms, parasites, diseases and spiritual problems.

If we hope to change the world for Christ then we must get off the sidelines and jump in the middle of the fight. We need to be salt in a barren land and a light shining bright offering hope to a world withering away in despair.

When we make that decision to join in the fight, we must remember what Paul said in 2 Corinthians 10:4, "The weapons we fight with are not the weapons of the world. On the contrary, they have divine power to demolish strongholds."

There are no problems in the world that we cannot overcome with the power of the Lord within us. Let me personally invite you to join us at Rivers of the World in our travels to some of the most remote regions—armed with the most effective weapon—the Word of God.

Give Wisely

We all have heard those ads pleading, "For just $39.95 a month your donation could send a child to school, provide them healthcare and feed them three times a day." Most of us are stirred when we see the empty eyes of a little child who appears to be malnourished or obviously in need of medical care.

The words used in these ads are great except for one word—could. If I am going to donate my hard-earned money then I don't want to know what my money could do in the life of a child. This only means my money might help a child attend school, may provide healthcare and possibly will feed a child.

I want to know specifically what exactly my money will do to ease the suffering in the lives of others. Striving to live like Christ will prompt us to be generous in our giving and to help others in need. We are told in Luke 6:38, "Give, and it will be given to you. A good measure, pressed down, shaken together and running over, will be poured into your lap. For with the measure you use, it will be measured to you."

As with any aspect of our lives, we should pray and seek the Lord's direction. We can be certain that if we give to others out of a sincere and generous heart, we shall be blessed. However, we should still take the time to study advertisements, including those in Christian magazines, and decipher whether the ads clearly state that your contribution will be used for a good cause or if it could be used for a good cause. Then, pray and ask for wisdom whether you should give, and if so, how much or in what way.

As a non-profit, Christian organization, we at Rivers of the World (ROW) will tell you plainly how your contributions are being used to provide medical care, education, and a host of other vitally necessary resources to people around the world. Most importantly, your donations allow us to travel to remote areas of the world and deliver the message of Jesus Christ.

God Almighty

The force behind a thunderstorm is quite different depending upon where you live. The magnitude of a thunderstorm in the Midwestern part of the United States is very different from a thunderstorm in the Southwestern part of our country. Likewise, a thunderstorm in Georgia, called a gulley washer or frog strangler, is also quite different.

The intensity of a thunderstorm in Cameroon in Central Africa is beyond what is common in the United States. The storm will shake you to your bones. The lightening will last for 20 seconds—the thunder just rolls on and on. The rain comes so hard you can't see through the wall of water. There is so much awesome power in a thunderstorm.

Recently, I read a very appropriate statement on a sign at a church that said, "Don't tell God how big the storm is, tell the storm how big your God is." There is a lot of truth and power in that statement.

In Revelation 1:8 (KJV), we can clearly see the power of our God—past, present and future. It says, "I am Alpha and Omega, the beginning and the ending, saith the Lord, which is, and which was, and which is to come, the Almighty."

Dear Christian, the next time you are facing a seemingly impossible situation, look up and know you serve an awesome, powerful and almighty God.

Good Stewards of the Earth

Contributions to Rivers of the World (ROW) have enabled us to support a laboratory in Lima, Peru where research is being conducted to reduce the threat of Malaria by getting rid of mosquitoes. Scientists have discovered a fascinating way to kill mosquito larvae without harming the environment.

The effects of Malaria is a real threat to people in this part of the world, who may experience fever, chills, nausea, muscle pain, and even death. The use of pesticides to control disease-carrying mosquitoes is not a healthy option for these delicate jungle environments. Instead, researchers have found a naturally occurring bacterium that is harmless to humans and animals, but kills the mosquito larvae.

The bacteria are actually commercially available, but its cost can be prohibitive for developing countries. A team of researchers at the University of Peru developed an inexpensive way to produce the bacteria by growing it in coconuts.

A small amount of the bacteria is dropped through a hole drilled in a coconut. The hole is then plugged and the bacteria then reproduce inside the coconut. After a few days, the coconuts are opened and poured into a mosquito-infested pond. The mosquito larvae eat the bacteria, which in turn kills the larvae by destroying its stomach lining.

The children in these remote Peruvian villages are being taught this technique of inoculating coconuts in order to reduce the threat of Malaria.

God not only created mankind, the air we breathe, the water we drink and all the animals that roam the face of the earth, He also created this unique bacterium which is reducing the spread of Malaria in remote jungle areas.

Our Lord has also instilled in us the wisdom and knowledge to discover answers to our problems in the environment in which we live. After God created Adam and Eve, He gave them dominion over the earth and instructed them to "subdue it (using all its vast resources in the service of God and man); and have dominion over the fish of the sea, the birds of the air, and over every living creature that moves upon the earth." (Genesis 1:28, Amplified Bible)

Let us go forth today and be good stewards of the earth that God created for humankind to enjoy for a season.

He Is Faithful

The year 2005 will be remembered as a very active deadly storm season. As Christ's return draws nearer, we see more hurricanes, torrential flooding, and devastating fires that sweep across our land. In the United States, we have accurate early warning systems that alert us to potential dangers of approaching storms.

In places like Bangladesh, these early warning systems do not exist. One farmer I know had to take his wife and five daughters and tie them in the top of coconut trees to ride out the worst storm of their lives.

After he got his family situated, the night fell and the rains came. I wonder what was going through his mind. "If something happens to my children, what will I do? If something happens to me, who will look after my family? If something happens to my wife, who will look after us?"

The next day following the storm, the sun rose, the farmer dug himself out from under his wet clothing, and discovered that his wife and all of his children had survived the storm.

In our lives, no matter how dark the night, how powerful the storm, the sun will surely rise again the next day and Jesus will still be Lord.

We can hold fast to His promise in Lamentations 3:22-23, which says, "Because of the LORD's great love we are not consumed, for his compassions never fail. They are new every morning; great is your faithfulness."

He Leadeth Me

Have you ever been lost? It happens to all of us from time to time. We are traveling on the road and suddenly we realize we have no idea where we are, nor do we have a clue how to find our way back to where we started. These incidences may be frustrating, but what is far worse is being utterly lost in our lives.

When I get lost, I am able to use many resources to assist me in my dilemma. I usually carry a map with me, which generally tells me where I am. I also carry a compass close by in my pocket or backpack or on the end of my knife. A compass at least shows me which direction is north. A Global Positioning System (GPS) is another tool that is useful in showing me longitude and latitude.

Usually, though, when I am lost I simply ask somebody for help. It usually works for me!

Where are you today? At this very moment are you lost or do you know where you are going?

If you are confused about decisions you must make in your life, let me encourage you to ask the Lord for direction. In Psalm 143:10 it states, "Teach me to do your will, for you are my God; may your good Spirit lead me on level ground."

When you come before the Lord, boldly ask Him to open or close doors and to show you distinctly and clearly the way that you should go. I can assure you if you pray this prayer with a pure heart and if you allow the Holy Spirit to lead, guide and direct you, He will indeed keep your feet on level ground and you shall not be led astray.

Holy Greetings

I'll see ya'll later! We Southerners have some interesting ways of saying hello and good-bye. This is true all over the world.

In India, people greet you by bowing slightly with their hands pressed together, palms touching in front of their chest, and saying "namaste." Translated, this means, "I worship the God I see in you," or, "the divine in me greets the divine in you."

There is also a beautiful greeting in Iraq that means, "Meeting you has been a holy experience."

How do most Americans greet one another? Do we simply say a quick, "hey" or "hello?" As Christians, we are to imitate our Lord and Savior in our words and actions. When we greet others, we should do so as if we were greeting Jesus himself. Make it a holy experience by saying things that are positive and encouraging. Lift your friends up with good comments, uplifting news and lots of hope.

Let us remind ourselves today of Hebrews 3:13 where we are instructed to "… encourage one another daily, as long as it is called Today, so that none of you may be hardened by sin's deceitfulness."

Greet someone today with exuberance, letting him or her know how wonderful it is spending time with them and how much they are cherished. It only takes a second to say something kind and uplifting and it may very well be the exact words someone needs to hear today.

Identify With Christ

Do you remember how the sign of the fish was used to identify Christians in ancient times? Today it seems like it's not very popular to be a Christian. In some of the countries I serve you can go to jail for being a believer. In other countries around the world, death is even a sentence served to those who follow Christ.

I think it is time, now remember that phrase, it is time for Christians to unite and create a new way to identify ourselves. With your left hand take your index finger and your middle finger and point it to the left of your body. That is exactly like the hands of a clock pointing to the time 3:16. Do you get it?

Christians, let us start a new movement to identify ourselves, to align our thoughts, words and deeds with our Lord and Savior Jesus Christ.

Now take those two fingers, point to the left of your body and if somebody points them back that means they're a believer and you're a believer and you both have a common bond in Jesus Christ.

The word of God in John 3:16 (KJV) says, "For God so loved the world, that he gave his only begotten Son, that whosoever believeth in him should not perish, but have everlasting life."

It is time, it is 3:16 and it is time for us to stand together as one and share the good news that God so love the world.

In Deed and in Truth

The dirt road was dusty as I walked along side an ancient African woman who spoke in her language and I spoke in mine. Down this path I learned that the woman's grandson had just died that day. She discovered that my two sons were still alive.

This ancient African woman's grandson had been placed on the floor of a mud hut with his arms folded across his chest. The seven-year-old boy's belly was swollen and his hair was gray. He had starved to death.

That day will forever be etched in my mind. It was the day I decided to care. Today, I want to ask you, "What would it take to make you care and for you to realize we can change the world one child at a time?"

In 1 John 3:18 (NKJV), we are warned, "... let us not love in word or in tongue, but in deed and in truth."

Christ is the very definition of love and truth and if He truly lives in your heart, you will feel compelled to help those in need by giving of your time, money and resources, all in the name of Jesus Christ. We can make a difference in this world by simply starting in our own neighborhood. The generosity and love we display to our neighbors will naturally flow outward and touch the lives of many others.

Little Is Much in Him

It is the little things that mean so much, isn't it? I am convinced that it is not the extravagant, grand efforts we make that are so compelling nor have the greatest impact. Instead, it is a kind touch, it is a pat on the back, a gentle word of encouragement, a "God bless you," and a simple prayer said for a friend in need.

The little, seemingly unobtrusive acts we do usually have the greatest impact upon a person's life. This was the case with Israel Gonzalez, who is a pastor in Honduras. He works in 15 villages. While visiting with Israel, we stopped in a home that had 15 people living under one roof. We entered the home and there were four little children and a mother. Everyone else was out doing work.

Unexpectedly, Israel miraculously made ice cream appear. To see the looks on the faces of those young children for such a kind and small gesture reminded me that it really is the little things that produce lasting results.

Paul instructs us in Colossians 3:12, "Therefore, as God's chosen people, holy and dearly loved, clothe yourselves with compassion, kindness, humility, gentleness and patience."

Christian, let me encourage you to daily look for ways to bless someone with an act of compassion, with a kind gesture or with a gentle word. These may seem like little deeds, but when conducted in the spirit of Christ, the deeds are multiplied into wonderful blessings.

No More Complaining

Just when we think our life is tough God graciously shows us a glimpse of a life much more difficult than our own. My own whining quickly subsided as I took part in a combat patrol with U.S. Marines in northern Iraq.

It was 3 a.m., windy, cold, wet and raining. In other words, it was absolutely miserable. We were slipping along looking for the enemy. This was a very frightening experience, for me. You know what I noticed on this patrol? Not one of these Marines complained, whined or acted afraid. They had been trained for these combat situations and they were simply doing their job to protect and preserve our freedom.

This glimpse of the conditions these Marines operate in reminded me that in my life my job as a Christian is to praise God and be thankful for all He has done. In Philippians 2:13-14, we are reminded, "for it is God who works in you to will and to act according to his good purpose. Do everything without complaining ..."

Regardless of your circumstances, set aside the whining and complaining and lift up your praises to the Lord. I would personally ask that you include in your daily prayers our young men and women who are serving overseas.

I was extremely proud to be with those Marines and especially one in particular, my son, Lt. Adam Mathes.

Praying To El-Shaddai
(God Almighty)

When you come before the throne of grace and present your petitions to God, what do your prayers sound like? Sometimes as I pray aloud to God, my prayers sound like I am whining, complaining or even begging. I forget about the most important aspects of prayer—the adoration and the praise. Most of all, I sometimes fail to remember the power of prayer.

This power was evident as I was on my knees along with 5,000 other people in the Congo. We were at a worship service that gathers in the middle of the afternoon on Sundays. It is not called church, but instead, spiritual combat.

People from all kinds of backgrounds come together in one accord and pray unto God. As the thousands of other people and I were pouring our hearts out to God, it sounded like a rainstorm on the tin roof above us. There was so much power as sin, fear, doubt and guilt were all washed away by the storm of that thunderous prayer.

In part, James 5:16 (KJV) says, "The effectual fervent prayer of a righteous man availeth much."

To understand this passage, we must fully comprehend the words "fervent" and "availeth." If someone is fervently praying, he or she is doing so with passionate enthusiasm. A better definition would be "unreservedly enthusiastic." In other words, we should come before El-Shaddai, God Almighty, the God who is sufficient for the needs of His people, and pour out our hearts completely with the knowledge that He is indeed all-powerful and capable of answering our prayers.

When we stand before God righteously in fervent prayer, His word says our prayers will "avail much." Our prayers will be effective—they will produce mighty results.

The next time you come before God in prayer, remember to first praise Him, not just for what He has already done and what He is about to accomplish, but merely for who He is—El-Shaddai. With a heart full of praise, we will be able to present our petitions to Him boldly and powerfully.

Priceless Possessions

I developed an unusual "friendship" in southern Belize while I was sharing a meal with a farmer in a small village. This was not an ordinary meal; it was a huge iguana. In many places in Central America you can find iguanas basking in the bright sunshine along the Caribbean. These lizards are believed to have medicinal value by curing or relieving various human ailments. The iguana's delicate white flesh is supposed to taste like chicken. Believe me, it is not very good!

After I shared a meal of iguana with this farmer, he decided we were friends and he took me into his hut. Very secretively, he reached under the bed and pulled out this treasure. It was a jade Mayan spear tip that was made in about 900 AD and worth a fortune. This new "friend" of mine asked me if I would smuggle the spear tip into America, sell it on the black market, and send him the money. I told him I was not about to take part in his plan and let him know that his treasure belonged to the people of Belize.

Fellow Christian, what are your three favorite treasures? How many of you just said your house, car and your money? Many of you probably thought your spouse and your children.

It is good to invest our time into meaningful pursuits and relationships, but I encourage you instead to follow the Lord's instructions in Matthew 6:19-21, "Do not store up for yourselves treasures on earth, where moth and rust destroy, and where thieves break in and steal. But store up for yourselves treasures in heaven, where moth and rust do not destroy, and where thieves do not break in and steal. For where your treasure is, there your heart will be also."

Today, determine to seek priceless possessions, such as Godly wisdom, compassion for lost souls, guidance from the Holy Spirit and Christ-like love for others.

Putting Things in Perspective

I just filled up my car with gas and boy did it take my breath away! If you are thinking about inviting me to your church, give me plenty of notice because I might just have to walk!

Putting things in perspective, we are blessed abundantly here in America. Some of our poorest people would be considered rich by the living standards of those occupying areas of Africa, South America and Central America.

Up in the mountains of Honduras there are 25 little kindergartens that have 15 students each and one teacher. Those teachers love these children so greatly that it is a moving experience to be with them. You would never know that these teachers receive a salary that is less than what it cost for us to fill up our vehicles every month with a tank of gas. It doesn't take much to change the world for Christ, but it does take some time, effort and resources.

Paul reminds us in Hebrews 13:16, "And do not forget to do good and to share with others, for with such sacrifices God is pleased."

The next time you fill up your vehicle with gas, instead of thinking about how much money you just spent, think instead about how you could take that same amount of money and do something good for the Lord to be a blessing unto others.

Rejoice in the Lord

Living in the South, meals are not just a time to eat, but also a time to fellowship with friends and family. Sometimes the food is good and sometimes it is not.

While overseas, we eat MRE's (Meals Ready to Eat), a staple diet of military personnel. The entrees are actually really good. The meals contain an ample supply of proteins, carbohydrates and calories to sustain you through the day. The meal kits also contain packets of crackers, cheese, peanut butter and salsa. In the Army, soldiers take all these extras, mix it together and chow down on what they call Ranger stew.

Life is very much like this—some good and some bad. We enjoy times of tremendous blessings and joy, while at other times we experience equally tremendous sorrow and disappointment.

The real tragedy is when we allow the heartaches and difficult times to consume us and block out the good that is around us. We reach a point after awhile where we drag through life just trying to survive and do the best we can, anyway we can.

God is clear in His word when he commands us in Philippians 4:4 to, "Rejoice in the Lord always. I will say it again: Rejoice!"

This is not an option. His word does not say to rejoice when life is full of wonder, excitement and happiness. Read the Scripture again, but this time focus upon what we are to rejoice in. It is not our circumstances, not the difficult time we are going through and not the pain we are feeling. We are to rejoice in the Lord. When we cannot see beyond our troubles to rejoice, then simply rejoice in who God is … sovereign, holy, faithful, ever-present and the very definition of love.

I encourage you to dedicate the rest of your life to making it a victory for Jesus Christ.

Serving Around the World

The boat had broken down and we had to hike out of the jungle. Our crew decided we would take whatever trail went up and if the trail forked, we would go to the left. We set out on our journey and finally made it to an old church where we spent the night on the floor.

The next day, our bush pilot located us and the first team was sent out. Thomas Webb and I waited for the last flight out. Our pilot, David, got us in the plane with all of our equipment and supplies. He then warned us that the plane might be overloaded. As the plane traveled down the runway, the pilot started screaming.

Thomas and I looked at each other and I said, "Well, this is it." As the plane barely cleared the trees, the pilot finished his scream by saying, "I just love this!" He scared us to death, but it reminded us of something—even if it is frightening, scary or a challenge, we just love serving our Lord around the world.

Whether you are a volunteer with Rivers of the World or serving as a missionary with your church, we are all called to share the good news of salvation to everyone—whether it is our next door neighbor, co-worker, someone in another state or in another country.

In Mark 16:15 we read, "He said to them, 'Go into all the world and preach the good news to all creation.'"

Today, I challenge you to step out of your comfort zone, set aside your fears, "go into your world," and tell everyone about the saving grace of God, the immeasurable love of Jesus Christ and the hope of eternity they can have through a personal relationship with our Lord.

Share Christ With Everyone

Dick Blakemore of Noblesville, Ind., God bless you! Dick, who looks a lot like Santa Claus on a bad day, reminded us of the necessity of sharing the Gospel with everyone. We were on the beach in Central America handing out Gospel tracts to all the Hispanic folks. As the people walked by, we handed them the tracts saying, "Here's the Word of God" in their native language.

Dick came up and asked, "Can I invite some folks to dinner?" We said, "Sure, who is it?" Dick then told us he had met two kids, one from France and one from Belgium, and he told them the Gospel story. He asked if they would like to eat dinner with us and said, "and they just may!'

Here we were in the middle of doing missionary work when Dick remembered the Gospel is to be shared with everyone in the world. Today, I encourage you to share the Gospel with everyone you meet.

In Luke 3:18 it says, "And with many other words John exhorted the people and preached the good news to them."

John the Baptist prepared the way for Jesus Christ. So, too are we to prepare the way for Christ's return by sharing the good news of salvation with everyone.

At Rivers of the World, it is our mission to share the love of Christ in word and deed.

Submit to Him

Are you a control freak? I learned a valuable lesson about what happens when you try to control too much.

I was on the Napo River in Peru for the first time when I became desperately ill. The crew put my tent on top of the ship and my staff was arguing about who was going to get my pants, my boots, and my knife when I was gone.

Thank goodness, Marcel Telders, affectionately known as "Doc," the Rivers of the World corpsman, kept me alive. My sickness did force me to turn over the expedition to Thomas Webb. I simply had to let go and allow God and Thomas to take care of my friends. They did a superb job.

If you are also a control freak, start this day by saying, "Lord, I give up trying to control it all. You take this day and you do with it what you want and I will rejoice in whatever comes my way." When we relinquish control of our lives to Christ, we will discover a tremendous amount of peace, strength and enthusiasm for the day.

Christ tells us in Luke 14:27, "And anyone who does not carry his cross and follow me cannot be my disciple."

When we choose to serve Christ and follow His ways, there is no neutral ground. Either we are serving Him, or we are not. We are either submitting to His ways and releasing control of our lives to Him, or we are not. Today, choose to give Him your all—your thoughts, your time, your obedience, your plans and every aspect of your life.

The Language of Love

There are some things in life that bring us together regardless of nationality or language, such as a common goal or a shared belief.

I was standing outside a refugee camp in Bangladesh when I saw a little boy wearing a watermelon on his head like a helmet and holding a badminton racket. This seemed perfectly normal to me so I walked up to the little child and said, "Oh, this is great! I wish you could speak English because there are so many things I'd love to ask you."

The main language spoken in Bangladesh is Bengali, which is also the second most commonly spoken language in India. More than 98% of the total population of Bangladesh speak Bengali as a native language.

Therefore, you can imagine my surprise when the little boy took the watermelon off his head and said, "Well, I say, we all speak English here. Don't you?"

I laughed and it reminded me that around the world Christians are bound together by the love of Jesus Christ and the fellowship of the Holy Spirit.

John encourages us and challenges us in 1 John 4:7-8 by saying, "Dear friends, let us love one another, for love comes from God. Everyone who loves has been born of God and knows God. Whoever does not love does not know God, because God is love."

The first thing we must realize is God is the very definition of love. As Christians, the Holy Spirit dwells within us and this love should be evident in all that we say and do. Whether we are fellowshipping with a Christian at our home church or a brother or sister in Christ from a world away, we all share that special bond of love only found through a relationship with Jesus Christ.

Today, you may be by yourself, but you are never alone because you are surrounded by those who will love you in the Lord.

Think Before You Speak

I took part in an interesting parade recently while touring the Wonju Christian Hospital in the province of Kangwon, located in central Korea. Taking part in this parade were nurses, interns, physicians and even the medical director of the hospital. The parade of people followed behind me as we went from floor to floor.

It is a very beautiful facility. Our tour led us to the audiology department where a young nurse was teaching a child who could neither hear nor speak how to communicate. The little boy learned to talk by feeling the vibrations in his throat. He stood before me and said, "How you doing preacher?"

The little boy then started crying, the nurse cried, I cried and we all wept together in hearing him communicate. This was a powerful moment. Don't you wish we all could take the time to think about every single word before we speak?

We are warned in Matthew 12:36-37, "But I tell you that men will have to give account on the day of judgment for every careless word they have spoken. For by your words you will be acquitted, and by your words you will be condemned."

I encourage you today to make a conscience effort to use your words in such a way that it brings honor and glory to the Lord. Make it a point to speak words of encouragement, hope and love to everyone whom you meet today.

Witness to the Ends of the Earth

By the time you read this I may be on my way to Al Hadithah, Iraq, located along the Euphrates River near the Syrian border. I'm striving to do all I can to gain permission to travel to northern Iraq to visit with our U.S. Marines and witness firsthand the great work these young people are doing on our behalf.

I don't want to be a silent observer, but instead, it is my heart's desire to preach to the troops and pray with these men and women who risk their lives daily for the freedom we enjoy here in America. By doing this, I will be in obedience to God's word where it states in Acts 1:8 (KJV), "But ye shall receive power, after that the Holy Ghost is come upon you: and ye shall be witnesses unto me both in Jerusalem, and in all Judaea, and in Samaria, and unto the uttermost part of the earth."

Might I add, unto Iraq, Afghanistan, Turkey, Egypt, India …

With this opportunity in Iraq, I want to share my adventures with listeners over the radio because I believe people need to hear, and I need to be reminded, of the wonderful things these young men and women are doing on our behalf in this region of Iraq. We are constantly bombarded with images of death and violence from the warfront of Iraq. I want to share the often overlooked images of courage, determination and sacrifice that define these Marines.

Selfishly, I hope to come across a particular lieutenant, Adam Mathes, for my name is Ben Mathes.

978-0-595-43261-5
0-595-43261-1

LaVergne, TN USA
21 September 2010
197756LV00003B/45/A